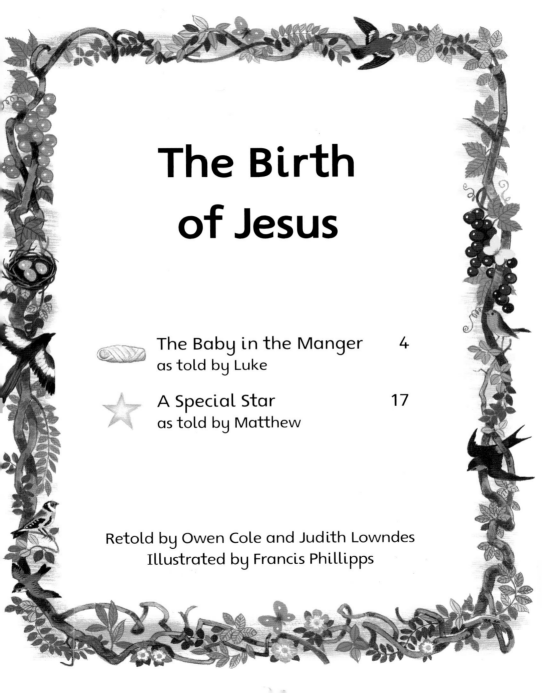

The Birth of Jesus

Retold by Owen Cole and Judith Lowndes
Illustrated by Francis Phillipps

Heinemann Educational Publishers
Halley Court, Jordan Hill, Oxford OX2 8EJ

MADRID   ATHENS   PARIS
FLORENCE   PRAGUE   WARSAW
PORTSMOUTH NH   CHICAGO   SAO PAULO
SINGAPORE   TOKYO   MELBOURNE   AUCKLAND
IBADAN   GABORONE   JOHANNESBURG

First published 1995

95 96 97 98 99 10 9 8 7 6 5 4 3 2 1

British Library Cataloguing in Publication Data
A catalogue record for this book is available from the British Library

Starter Pack
1 of each of 12 titles: ISBN 0 435 01066 2

Library Hardback Edition
The Birth of Jesus: ISBN 0 431 07753 3
1 of each of 12 titles: ISBN 0 431 07763 0

Designed by Sue Vaudin; printed and bound in Hong Kong

Acknowledgements
Back cover photograph:
Madonna and Child (detail) by Duccio, early 14th century,
Bridgeman Art Library

Many, many years ago a special
baby was born.
His name was Jesus.
Here are two stories about his birth.

 # The Baby in the Manger

There was a good and kind lady called Mary.
One day a very strange thing happened.
Mary saw a bright light in her room.
In the middle of the light was an angel.

Mary was very scared.

The angel said, "Do not be scared Mary.
I have come to tell you that you will
have a very special baby."

The angel said, "When the baby grows
into a man, he will be a great leader."
Mary began to think hard about
what the angel had said.

Mary's husband was called Joseph.

Mary and Joseph had to go to

a town called Bethlehem.

It was a long way.

When they got to Bethlehem there were lots of people there.

There was nowhere for Mary and Joseph to stay.

It was time for Mary to have her baby.

Mary and Joseph found a place to rest.
Mary had her baby.
She wrapped him up and put him in
a manger where the animals eat.

That same night some men were looking
after their sheep in the hills near
Bethlehem.
All was quiet.

Suddenly there was a very bright
light in the sky.
The men were scared.
"What is it?" they cried. "What is it?"

In the bright light stood an angel.

"I have good news," said the angel.

"A special baby has been born in
Bethlehem.

Go and visit him."

Then the sky was full of angels.

The men were very scared.

They heard the angels sing about the
very special baby.

"What shall we do?" said the men.

"Let's go and find the special baby,"
they said.

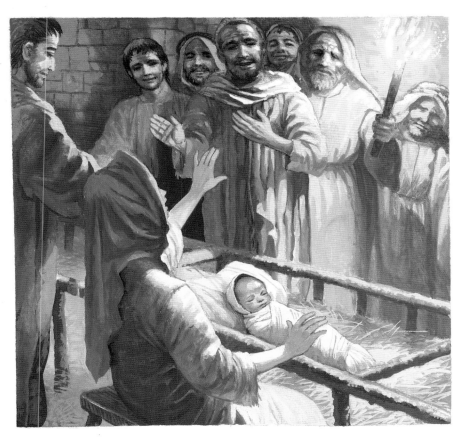

They found the baby in the manger.
They told Mary and Joseph about the
angels.
They told them that the angels said that
the baby was special.

Then they went back to their sheep.

They were very happy.

They had seen the baby Jesus.

A Special Star

There was once a good man called Joseph.
He was going to marry a lady called Mary.
One night Joseph had a strange dream.

In his dream an angel spoke to Joseph.
The angel said, "When you marry Mary
she will have a special baby.
You will call the baby Jesus."

So Joseph married Mary and she did
have a baby.
They called the baby Jesus because
the angel told them to.

Far away some men were looking at
the stars in the sky.

They saw a new star.

They said, "This star means that a king
has been born."

The men set off to find the new king.
They went to the king's palace to
look for the baby.
But the baby Jesus was not in the palace.

The men followed the star until
it stopped over a house.
They went into the house.

They found baby Jesus and
his mother, Mary.
They bowed down in front of Jesus.

They gave him special gifts.

They had found the special baby.

They went home and were very happy.